*Escaping the House of Certainty*

SUSAN LUDVIGSON

## *Escaping the House of Certainty*

*Poems*

LOUISIANA STATE UNIVERSITY PRESS

BATON ROUGE

This publication is supported in part by an award from the National Endowment for the Arts.

Published by Louisiana State University Press
Copyright © 2006 by Susan Ludvigson
All rights reserved
Manufactured in the United States of America
First printing

Designer: Laura Roubique Gleason
Printer and binder: Edwards Brothers, Inc.
Typefaces: Jansen Text, Matrix Script Display
Typesetter: G&S Typesetters, Inc.

Grateful acknowledgment is made to the editors of the following publications, in which the poems listed first appeared: *Antioch Review*, "Christmas in the Officer's House" (Winter 2002); *Cold Mountain Review*, "In the House" (Fall 2001); *Crazyhorse*, "A Woman Enters a Garden Through Cornfields" (Winter 2002); *Georgia Review*, "The Invisible Is Not Lost" (Fall 2001); *Gettysburg Review*, "Chalabre" (Spring 1998), "The Family of Man" (Fall 2002); *Kestrel*, "Mushrooms in the Style of the Aude" (Spring 2002); *Lake Effect*, "Parfait Voice," "Montaillou," "Gratin Dauphinoise" (all Spring 2006); *Left Bank*, "A female boar stands silent, grazing" and "I do not know him" (both forthcoming); *Mid-American Review*, "Tautavel" (Fall 1998); *Ohio Review: New and Selected, 1971–2001* (2001), "Puivert," "Summer Fruit Dessert," "Aioli," "Puivert 2," "Charleston"; *Pedestal Magazine*, "On Love and Murder," "Floating the Lynches River in October," "Discoveries in a Morning Diary" (all March 2001); *Pleiades*, "Improvisation under Moonless Tectonics" (Spring 2002); *Poet Lore*, "Barcelona, the Spanish Civil War" (Winter 2004); *Southern Poetry Review*, "Sundae in the Pyrenees" (Spring/Summer 2004); *Southern Review*, "It Is Because of the One Body She Tells Us" (Summer 2003); *21st: The Journal of Contemporary Photography*, ed. John Wood, "Danse Macabre" (Vol. IV), "Phantoms" (Vol. VI); *Water/Stone*, "To Know What Takes Us" (Spring 2002); *Yemassee*, "It Tells You" (Spring 2000).

"Escaping the House of Certainty" first appeared in *A Millennial Sampler of South Carolina Poetry*, ed. Gilbert Allen (Greenville, SC: Ninety-Six Press 2005). "Bin Laden in South Carolina" appeared previously in the *Gettysburg Review* (Fall 2002); *A Millennial Sampler of South Carolina Poetry*, ed. Allen; and *Twenty: South Carolina Poetry Fellows*, ed. Kwame Dawes (Spartanburg, SC: Hub City Writers Project 2005).

Library of Congress Cataloging-in-Publication Data
Ludvigson, Susan
Escaping the house of certainty : poems / Susan Ludvigson.
    p. cm.
ISBN-13: 978-0-8071-3184-8 (cloth : alk. paper)
ISBN-10: 0-8071-3184-9 (cloth : alk. paper)
ISBN-13: 978-0-8071-3185-5 (pbk. : alk. paper)
ISBN-10: 0-8071-3185-7 (pbk. : alk. paper)
I. Title.
PS3562.U27E73   2006
811'.54—dc22

2006010398

The paper in this book meets the guidelines for permanence and durability of the Committee on Production Guidelines for Book Longevity of the Council on Library Resources. ∞

For Scott

*Contents*

**1**

It Tells You   3
The Invisible Is Not Lost   4
It Is Because of the One Body She Tells Us   5
To Know What Takes Us   6
Everything to Do with How We Entered   7
Dreams/Villages 1
   Puivert   8
   Chalabre   8
   Belesta   8
Mushrooms in the Style of the Aude   9
A Woman Enters a Garden through Cornfields   10
The Geometry of Drowning   11
Aioli   12
Dreams/Villages 2
   Ax les Thermes   13
   Tautavel   13
   Puivert 2   13
Café, Early Morning, Paris   14
On Love and Murder   15
Eggplant Provençal: A Homily   17
Anywhere Outside Paris   18
Sundae in the Pyrenees   19
At the New Year   20

**2**

Improvisation under Moonless Tectonics   25
Floating the Lynches River in October   28
Rice Lake Soup   29

A Little Night Music   30
Dreams/Villages 3
  Puivert 3   31
  Falling in Love in Camon   31
  Parfait Voice, Montaillou   31
In the House   33
Dreaming My Mother in the Bone Church, Kostnice   34
Summer Fruit Dessert   36
Charleston   37
French Bread   38
Labyrinths   39
Discoveries in a Morning Diary   40
Gratin Dauphinoise   41
She Makes Another Comeback   42
Dreams/Villages 4
  Esperaza   43
  Mirepoix   43
  Collioure   43
Someone Who Believes Herself Native   45
Escaping the House of Certainty   46

# 3

Amnesia   49
The Family of Man   50
Phantoms   53
Christmas in the Officer's House   54
Moroccan Tuna   55
Barcelona, the Spanish Civil War: Alfonso Laurencic Invents Torture by Art   56
We Do Not Notice   57
Again the Thickness of the Night   58
I Thought I Knew You   59
Bin Laden in South Carolina   60

# 4

Danse Macabre   65

*1*

We paint thick lines
around the body, trust the brush
to say what will be allowed inside,
what must circle like a hawk
perpetually hungry.

## *It Tells You*

Your body knows better than you what it needs.
    —Marguerite Yourcenar

It knows how the moon floats over dreams
the way a tree rides a November sunset.
The glowing body never lies.
It doesn't fan itself, hiding
a smile while it flashes its eyes,
nor does it indulge in innuendo.
The body glides on truth. Its gaze
seldom wavers. Even when it chooses
discretion, it gives itself away.
Think of a hawk drifting slowly down,
hunger riding its wings, the suddenness
with which drift segues into dive.

## *The Invisible Is Not Lost*

       Before the dictionary
               the blood translates on its own       finds
            a way to light
       a caffeine quickening      or a sword
                  thinking it has breath
        perhaps what it means to the body
             an electric return      a moving
shock
    waterfall into crescendo

               things that never leave us
               in any country
      October moon
               one foot over the horizon

## *It Is Because of the One Body She Tells Us*

              let ideas ragged from lack of sleep circle as they will
       intact

                 all the bones deliberate
          inhale white morning
                  inside its sheath
cells hum nearby
     unaware of clouds behind the clouds
            lying in a hammock      warm October
                  mums ranged rust and yellow

the heart lulled

                    a casual meeting
             as in a stranger's eyes
      assumption darkens to crimson

    young
           I taught myself to Roman ride     to stand on my bay's back
as he galloped through the grain
                  became another

      it is not age that makes us     ask
          that makes us wish to cradle
                what we are

## *To Know What Takes Us*

                   forget the rules            a funnel of shadow
an ache       nothing dramatic
                         goes by many names     all of them
       in your peripheral vision                   whispered
    try to pronounce something not quite alarming
            what you fear will turn on you     you'll begin to feel queasy
as something rocks in on a wave that knocks you over
   you swallow                      you wouldn't call it pain
        it is only water            but you forget how to swim

what do we ask for in the new life
    what do we answer
                      descending       with the sun
           as it slips through that cuff

     you should be sleeping
        you have taken the pills and everything is becoming one thing
  since long before the last dawn
    the stage is lowering       out of sight       clay
beneath the orchestra pit
              .     if there's a groan it's muffled by drums

## *Everything to Do with How We Entered*

Canter of bombs,
delicate bones over a roof.
The playhouse moves, a gray ripple,
no longer mine. What leads us through
the erotics of memory? Miraculous brain,
after song, after years of chemicals,
lilacs dusty against a palm, the coded dark
listening. Voices, smooth palomino,
echo all the way to the river. June:
sure quick peonies, small blue cupboard, blue
sharpened by war, and the blue crib
with a name etched on the headboard.
Lost behind saddles. Where the icehouse
sat and leaves piled in the street.
Where the grain was stored oat-smell
burns fragrant, the way everything returns—
apples, frost so close we gave ourselves
permission. The way the latch locked
and opened.

# Dreams/Villages 1

### Puivert

Bats are looping the air, ink-sweeps against the moon, not words but elegant thoughts, our neighbor might say, who likes them, speaks of softness, the way it feels to the palm to stroke them. When one swoops in from the balcony, I am not charmed. I fly downstairs, lock myself in the closet. It follows me down, circles the bedroom. Finally it descends another floor and my husband shuts the basement door, tells me it's safe to come out. But he's wrong—one clings to my shoulder, my breasts, its eyes peer into mine. I think of smashing it with something hard, instead brush it off into air. I am relieved, three times turn the lock in the door. Now balcony walls are white with pink blossoms, effortless shapes alive in the moonlight, a sway against stone.

### Chalabre

Outside the village, an old man sits on a hill every day, his lawn chair leaning into the green while he reads, unaware of the cars passing before him. There's a view of sunflowers, plane trees, mountains soft enough in the haze to make him sleepy, but he does not look up. In his book, soldiers approach, they surround a town fortified by walls not yet ancient, not crumbling. One wears a red plume in his helmet, has a woman by the arm. Her cries shatter the air before him. In the background, music plays, a kind of flute, and tents go up as the sun slides down. He does not notice the heat as it diminishes. Now the soldier takes the woman into a tent, the sounds are muffled. A breeze ruffles the grass, the light deepens.

### Belesta

We are searching under September trees for mushrooms—chanterelles only, no *rouges*, nothing exotic. One among us had eaten a poisonous kind last summer and barely survived. Confident now, he directs me to a secret hollow. He has taken a day off from hefting and carving marble, to lead us. Wherever I move in the grove, I hear hooves beating the ground, a herd gone wild. I run away from the sound, flee deeper into the forest. When I stop, out of breath, in a clearing, my pulse is a drum roll. The trees enclose a circle of sculpture: inside that ring, the mushrooms are red. The horses have gathered.

# *Mushrooms in the Style of the Aude*

    wild French mushrooms called *rouges;* if not available, any capped
       mushrooms, preferably wild
    sea salt
    the best olive oil you can find

*Have a barbecue, fireplace, or campfire prepared with very hot coals.*

In mushroom picking we must remember that we are not gods. What they can eat with impunity and pleasure, we must test by more accurate measures than silver coins in a pot. Here's how you produce, in minutes, cups of such delight they transform themselves into wisdom overnight. Lay clean mushroom caps on a narrow grate, their smooth roundness down. Think of them as chalices. Into each, pour a spoonful of olive oil, its gold blending with the rose of delicate skin, already suggesting translucence. Sprinkle salt into the openings, over the oil. The four elements of antiquity are about to come together. Salt from the sea = water. Oil from a tree = earth. Over coals you've tended to a glow, place the grate, watching fire leap softly up to join with air. Now: a lusciousness on the lips you won't be prepared for; lusciousness those who guard the secret of their mushroom troves swear they'd be willing to die for.

# *A Woman Enters a Garden through Cornfields*

                                    into moonlight

           where orchids wait         or *were* they cornfields?
              and still with infinite patience         the moon
I see them against dark walls in orbit
                moments         forests made of color         light-striped
                  the garden becomes
       or has not been written
              the garden         the orchid containing every other
the way human couples      the way we
         when blossoms encompass         everything
                  electric
              we say chemistry
   of all the billions
            when I wake in a dream knowing what
we could be showered by     it's only one of a series of wakings
   how often we see faces        we can navigate
      one world
                     another

## *The Geometry of Drowning*

She is enamored with pattern
                treads water
                              walks into a rhombus of red
                                                  gold

          and then the miracle
                            she rises
entering the world
                                    on her own thought

                    flying cities      delectable lives
     where she'd been lost
           found
              the shapes
                  of a dozen grain fields      waves
         in the pond    the German Shepherd
                      swimming
                                ovoid swamp with cattails
                late summer where
            the shadows of unlit candles
        she is leaning toward

                      depend

## *Aioli*

You've always wondered, haven't you, what the big deal could be about a mayonnaise. Well, the troubadours, one story claims, derived their inspiration from it when the female objects of their adoration were exhausted—exhausted, of course I mean, as muses: they were chaste as violets, all of them. And probably you know that it's the sacred sauce around which festivals in southern France have sprung. All I can tell you is this—it's easier than pie, and if you haven't, you must try it. Toss two egg yolks in your Cuisinart (yes, I could say processor, could be more sensitive to other manufacturers, but poets, even troubadours, have always done their best to reject the generic—and if you pronounce Cuisinart as the French do, it even makes a romantic music) with four rough-chopped cloves of garlic. Through the feed-tube (a term neither those ancient poets nor I could be happy to inscribe) gently, slowly, pour two cups of excellent mild olive oil—not green but the gold of a southern sun, and the juice of one smallish lemon. Place the aioli in a bowl and, on a large platter, surround it with whatever you think might fall in love with it—asparagus, cherry tomatoes, new potatoes, boiled eggs, sliced rare beef, cold poached fish (think salmon), handsome men with swords at their sides, women in silk, fanning themselves. Use, I want to say, your imagination. You too may be chaste, or want people to think so, but you don't want to give the impression that you're an aioli virgin.

# Dreams/Villages 2

### Ax les Thermes

Last year Josephine's bicycle slipped on the gravel, crashed into a plane tree. She flew, arms and legs spread like a blind angel. Diastole, systole, she chants as she enters the healing waters. No, her blood pressure is fine, but the words remind her of the hospital, the days that passed in dream, that music in her veins, before she knew her legs were stone. After the baths, she wants to go to the playground, to be lifted into a swing. When the sun sweeps her face she dips and rises in and out of shade. The years might be undone, she'll close her eyes and become who she never was.

### Tautavel

Near Tautavel the skeletal face of a man was found, carbon-dated 455,000 years. The museum's reconstruction shows thick folds over his eyes that made him nearly blind. He must have leaned into sound, danger announcing itself with a buzz, or the way a presence unsettled the trees. The body still knows the world by sound, sometimes nearly imperceptible. Invisible antennae pick up everything around it. Think of Victor Hugo, who could hear ants and moles tunneling underground. And what about the noise we produce ourselves, inside? Is there a monitor, a way to stay on track? Sometimes I hear my cells dreaming, and underneath it all, the dirge of bones.

### Puivert 2

The chic people from Marseilles arrive, then local guests—some in jeans, some in cotton skirts, two in low-cut sequined dresses. A few carry babies in their arms, sleeping or wailing. But the wedding is delayed: the bride's daughter, Isabel, has had an attack of *foie*. We wait in our car—it's air-conditioned. Some stand in the shady hall, others mill in the *place* and chat and sweat. In half an hour the girl recovers. We all crowd into the marriage room of the Mairie. The reception, outdoors, is noisy. As the band warms up, I hear someone say *"les anges,"* a fragment of conversation. But the choir is not angels. Floating above us, crows, an onerous singing.

# Café, Early Morning, Paris

A girl tucks blonde hair
                       under a red wool hat
       once she didn't think of men at all      disgusting
    she shouldn't be here
         above the door                  grapes hang in clusters
     the girl with her lover
           their sexual parts appear
  in clouds      in narrow lanes
                          of plane trees
       cannot seem to talk
the tangled vines
         she glimpses             her own wishes
      the bird she held
              the way
    her hands look
empty       even if the bush
                whose branches gnarl
      even if the bush     conceals
     she can't be sure
           she tells how a man    slid her silk dress off
     a waiter opening once
          and ever since     between his knees
    the big clock
in the corner
                drawing the cork out gradually
   ticks in her ear
     with his simple tool
        the pendulum swinging

# On Love and Murder

Sometimes you wake knowing you've murdered a baby
    *What is not metaphorical*
 *is not*    nobody knows   has ever known

    I was divorced years ago
but now you feel the police had never  another man
     intervened  getting close
    you're panicked
 guilty   you can't
    end   and the life that began
     a dream in a church—
  an accident
    your heart leaves and returns
 you might be the body's heaven

    the woman recently arrested  her child
   in the lobby of the mind
     mummified in a closet for twenty years
   his hands on my breasts  so I asked him
 to recite   crudely
     the smell was kept at bay with spices
 Plato  Socrates in the bed  wrapped even more tightly
     the police did finally find her
    he decided he should
  after all
   change rooms  you can't imagine how or why you know
      this was not the first time
    love draped me like this
   anything happens  not once  but over and over

    days anybody else would see as common
       daisies in the back yard
  her grave shallow too
   in a field

    the shade a cardinal makes—
                    when it flies over they are coming for you
         and guilt is finally
            the mesh
      I could neither breathe nor see without

# Eggplant Provençal: A Homily

    4 medium eggplants
    1 green bell pepper
    1 red bell pepper
    1 yellow bell pepper
    4 Tbsp. mayonnaise
    3 Tbsp. finely chopped red onion
    1 garlic clove, finely chopped
    1 pinch cayenne
    salt and pepper
    12 black olives (imported)
    2–3 tomatoes
    1½ tsp. lemon juice

*Serve at room temperature; 6 servings.*

An eggplant, you might not have guessed, is imagination in disguise. It reminds us of the potential of our lives. When we take it in, the soul rejoices, along with the tongue, surprised. What seemed impossible is possible again. Gather the eggplants and peppers and put them, whole, in a pan together under the broiler or over a grill, and let them char—another reminder of how life sometimes scars. Keep turning them gently, with tongs, until they're black. Take peppers off the fire first, popping them into a plastic bag, and seal it tight, letting them steam (not stew, exactly), to bring the metaphor around, in their own juices. When they're cool enough to handle, peel off skins, discard seeds, moodiness, and irritability. Chop them, not too small, and mix them with the mayonnaise (home-made is preferable, of course, but the best you can buy will be fine) and onion, hot pepper and garlic. When they're soft, slice the darkened eggplants in half carefully—think of yourself as helping something hatch—and with a spoon, lift out what's inside. Chop the eggplant too and add it to the mixture you've started. Salt and pepper. Stir well, and just before serving stir again, adding the lemon juice. Mound in the middle of a platter, letting it be the center of attention, as it desires, and around it arrange olives, black, to remind us where we've been, and wedges of ripe tomato, to awaken our sense that the world is growing brighter. What we'll discover is that *we* are new and as lovely as we were meant to be. Recall that the eggplant dresses like royalty.

# Anywhere Outside Paris

                                        a horse
           throws me off
                                    the hinterlands
                              spring whole out of snow
                        dangerous hooves
                 crack in cold air
   leather                    booths
                     my café       The Cluny
          so close I can feel      over coffee and notebook
                       a breath on my ear
                   a scarf of will
                                a dark loosely tied
          order of mind
                      my throat close
                                  his teeth
            I can't
                re-enter the dim-lit
                   the gauzy blue
                 except through erasure

can't hear but can sing          in sleep         on a page
           notes like this
                                 releasing his grip
                       tomorrow silk becomes sky
                            creeps up      makes an island

## Sundae in the Pyrenees

> goat cheese, soft, mild, like Montrachet
> honey
> mint leaves

When you have more money than time, more wish to simplify than to expand your culinary mind, here's a dessert both satyrs and saints adore. It's an aphrodisiac, and pure as the first village snow. Be profligate, buy as much of this delicate cheese as you can. What you don't use you can freeze. Just remember, it doesn't mind the cold, but wants to come back to a warm room's softness before offering itself to you. Scoop it into crystal bowls and pour the honey lavishly over. Go ahead, it's even good for you. Think of it as gold you should spend on yourself in order to learn how to live—lazily, slow. Decorate with mint leaves, a sprig or two. This voluptuous dish is not even sinful, though if that would make it better, you're welcome to think so.

## At the New Year

*You ask too many questions     you expect too much*
                    you say to that ribald servant who runs the house

              when someone demands perfection of herself
in the immodest palace of her mind
                        that someone is you
         especially
                decked out for the body's Christmas

who are we to ask big questions
                         we know now            in any bargain
         we made
                      back when belief was children holding hands
   was a chain snaking easy
      that we must learn          really learn
    to coil that many times around earth
         to eat our daily
              bread and toast with joy
      gratitude a ball of string
                        but when you said *earth* to your colleague
              who nearly died
a year ago today
                weren't you talking about
         the universe
                         glad to grade papers     glad to charge a dead
battery
                who doesn't get them confused          for that
       matter       to take your spaniel to the vet
      to have your loves
                  mingled in the confines of a single room

              can be all of it         so why are you
      bringing home stories of accidents

     jotted notes
for places outside your skin
      do you think of dreams
    as if they were proof
      do you believe you'll find something
   better than the self unwinding
     don't forget Emily   everything pales
            next to being alive

## 2

A female boar stands silent, grazing.
Do boars graze? Who told me to come here?
She runs toward me, I'm leaning
against a tree, her head is down, but I
do not draw back. She stops,
closes her eyes, as I close mine.
She breathes my breath,
I hers. We stand like that a while.
We stand like that.

# *Improvisation under Moonless Tectonics*

1

And what if it should begin
           in a corner
like this one

where we had not thought

       it could      what if colors
    suddenly frame a room

we've tiptoed into safely, black and white, the way
          we learned over time
               and time distinguished us

Japanese maples
      in a wheat field
          few and unexpected rewards

                         the flour sacks women made

      into dresses       stories we suspected
     were fictions
and stepmothers
     whose children ate bananas
          while the others

remembered
       and after that
           the rooms they couldn't
enter   the rooms they would never enter

**2**

    Is it auspicious               this
                        way of approach
          blindness
     attached to machines       the brain
        getting it

the way once it was the body            alone
          tools so
   crude it seemed only the body
beside me        everything I could want
          to know
             beneath everything
     I need for love

     a cocoon broken open
              letters lying on a branch    falling
the self impressed
       with rawness
everywhere
       sounds of the city

**3**

Afterward
        everything goes dandelion
              goes milkweed

      lost in the moment

you run naked
        a phrase
      flattening like grass
     in low wind         an immediate
                                            path
        abandoned


                a snag       purple thistle in
the psyche             while it sifts
     that knowledge that

       caress

# *Floating the Lynches River in October*

Day of the pileated woodpecker
                                              chasing a hawk
                  ducks rising heavily in twos        then threes
    But that's not                I want to say        how rings of light
keep falling down a tree trunk
                    rings ceaselessly
      as onto a finger
                leaves
                    overlapping

        a jet flies straight up
      stream of semen                          sky deep
              dizzying
         like standing close
to a cliff is
        then fallen trees     a series of crossings out
            we slip under    heads bent
              safe water:
       mussel shell open, hinged, iridescent
            still on the floor of the canoe
     did I say hornet's nest?
               hangs above us     huge
                        heart against the blue

# Rice Lake Soup

1½ c. chopped scallions, including some green parts
3 c. sliced wild mushrooms, fresh, or dried and reconstituted; a variety
⅓ c. butter
⅓ c. flour
8 c. chicken broth
¾ c. wild rice, cooked according to pkg. directions
¾ c. whole milk
¾ c. heavy cream
3 Tbsp. dry sherry
3 tsp. salt
3 Tbsp. chopped parsley

*8 servings*

Should you find yourself, of a November evening, longing for a life before your birth when, moccasined, you'd tread the leaf-soft earth to stalk your meat—maybe caribou or squirrel—close your eyes and will it. You can return to paradise, where rice grew wild in lakes just off birch-lined shores, where the law says this wild rice can be harvested only by Americans native to this land. Today we'll be those earlier men and women. With sharpened stones we'll chop wild onion (or scallions), slice mushrooms gathered in the woods two months ago. Instead of bear fat, harder to come by now, cook the above in butter, covered, for 10 minutes; then, the fire low, uncovered for 5 more. Instead of rough-ground cornmeal, I prefer plain flour, which you'll add and stir from time to time, 3 minutes in addition. Should you have it handy, use mallard stock; if not, chicken will do nicely. Add and cook for several minutes, about 10. You'll want to see the broth begin to thicken. Then stir the wild rice in along with venison drippings, if you especially like them, or milk and cream—an unusual but lovely substitute. You may prefer the juice from boysenberries—I use dry sherry. Add salt and bring to a simmer. That's all. Pour into your best glazed bowls—blue—to remind you of the lake outside the cabin in your mind. Toss on some parsley. More important: Remember where you are and how you got here. Welcome home.

# A Little Night Music

        Words                        not pitch or orchestration
                                                              I heard
                Strindberg and Bergman
    waterfalls
          krumkaker     orange-chocolate      at Christmas
lutefisk and lefse

                          Kiersten cartwheeling       in the kitchen
     a drifter gulping coffee
              soirées filled with desire      *comme les fleurs* drifting
folding the night into layers
                                           pure as accidental ballet
         the rise and letting go      of breath
                    the echo over the echo
                                    blurred

# Dreams/Villages 3

### Puivert 3

The famous director is here, a decade after he made the movie that made him friends with our grocer's son, now "Cook to the Stars." He's visiting Richard and showing his new film. Maybe because we're American, he tells us his secret: he is in love with Eve Arden. This morning he meanders through the village, through the untended orchard next to the road, then sits in Jacqueline's garden, talks of passion. They should have had a child, he says. The pears on the trees are just beginning to ripen. America is a dream, he goes on, its women prim but under the starch, swollen with ardor. He likes the schoolmarm voice, a woman with authority. He called her on the telephone, said, Miss Brooks, come to Puivert, come to the Pyrenees. I'm here alone, my life still made of longing. She tells him, as he knows she will, Bertie, don't be silly. He tosses his soft hands, palms to the sky, leaves the next morning.

### Falling in Love in Camon

A parrot has joined us for dinner, his feathers meticulous, his red tail smoothed, though the overhead fan makes that scarlet move in a rhythm like dancing. He is urbane, his conversation witty, as if we're in a movie, I think, supposing all his lines rehearsed. But they are neither rote nor imitation. He's a philosopher, his ideas are original. My mother is charmed, and my sister. Even my brothers smile at his jokes. I say, "I'll bet you've had better meals than this." He raises one emerald wing to call a waiter, laughs, sipping Blanquette de Limoux before admitting yes, he has, but never found the company more attractive. He turns his golden eyes on me. I feel the colors of him rippling rainbows in my blood. The family, predictably, frowns no. Except my sister, Mary Jo, who understands— who knows.

### Parfait Voice, Montaillou

A violet voice calls, sweet and tart, the voice of a sister or a mother. Perfect love, with its cloves and coriander, you think. Its lemon and vanilla. Here is a spirit you can take into yourself, a voice carrying Easter in its upper register. And a fragrance so old that if someone had asked, you'd say you'd forgotten. But you are returned to another body, lithe and limber, a trick-rider's body. You might go out in an hour to stand on a sorrel mare's back, to gallop through fields that carry this moment. If you'd lived in twelfth-century France, it would be the voice of a priest, a *parfait*. He'd come in his threadbare robe to tell you not to count on this joy, its blithe assumptions.

## *In the House*

        In the house with insects hatching        everything reappears as if
you had not        written and crumpled     a swarm
                              aims at your thigh
        surrounds me     the screen had not been locked
   the house of my father and my mother    moments ago was white
look at my thigh now covered    at the crucial moment    when will I know
              not to disturb         a hive
    with round welts    a scattering    as one should expect
 you were trying to say    you said    behind every shadow
a mosaic of glass       you were in the house where
      brilliant colors    scattered    insects hatching
   secrets    against the skin    translucent
                    I might be wearing a church window
    I tell them    photographs    a small explosion
  Look at my thigh    now covered
    stained glass brilliant redsyellowsblues

          believe in this catastrophe
            in each    a collage    the same people    pale skin
                  the chemicals        not fixed
                        everything returning

## *Dreaming My Mother in the Bone Church, Kostnice*

Five years after her death,
I take her hand, lead her
onto a dance floor.

A door opens, a breeze flits through,
and the chandelier sings,
throat bones dangling
crystal, finger bones
keeping time.

Ringed with skulls,
woven white wrists
warp and woof a loose
call to mass
note by clicking note.

Death is the mother of beauty,
we've been told, and here,
a few miles from Prague,
the woodcarver Frantisek Rindt,
commissioned by monks
to transform the remains
of 40,000 dead
into "pleasing arrangements," did.

For this grace,
her body doesn't need
what was once her mind.
We glide near

the coat-of-arms bones
studded with knuckles
rosaries of knuckles
vases and crosses, chalice

and pyramid of hip bones.
In falling light,
fibias swirl.

Her blue skirt flares
as she twirls. We skim

through arches and doorways
toward fleur-de-lys bones,
bones of the toes making roses.
As the sun comes up slowly
in South Carolina, in March,
I wake to my life
in a strange contentment.

Is there anything left to wish for?

# Summer Fruit Dessert

2 c. strawberries and blueberries, mixed
2 pears
1 seedless orange
2 Tbsp. orange juice
3½ Tbsp. confectioner's sugar
2½ Tbsp. Grand Marnier
2 Tbsp. amaretto
1 Tbsp. Framboise
1 small pinch curry

We're into easy here. It's summer and the markets are dressed in motley. The day of a parade you haven't time to make a *tarte*, though tarts abound (look around the square) and you might, for a day or a night, want to be one. Listen: the marionettes are singing ancient love songs. Gather your rosebuds if you wish, but a dessert of fruits will be a fillip to even such fêtes as begin with kir and end in bed. Somewhere in between, gather strawberries, blueberries, pears, plump sections of orange. Slice the pears into silvery wisps of moon and add the bright orange crescents, the juice, and the hulled, rinsed berries, too. They'll stay fresh if they think snow is falling, fooled by your sprinkling of powdery sugar and put for an hour in the fridge. Now: amaretto, Grand Marnier, Framboise. Toss them into that mélange of color. Did I mention the secret ingredient? Curry. It's good in nearly everything, a pinch so small it's undetectable, but it adds a certain *je ne sais quoi*, the way you'll feel when you taste each liqueur as you add it. Stir, and there you have it—sweet, voluptuous ending to an Audoise summer evening.

## *Charleston*

To let a horse loose in a wilderness of eighteenth-century houses, in the dark, is to risk more than you thought. Black, black, is the horse against the pitched sky as he gallops the Battery's walkway. Through cobblestone streets he clatters and weaves as if pole-bending, heading for anywhere open. Then north, toward one of the bridges. I find him, he's near the Cooper River, he finds me, now I am riding, saddleless, trying to guide him, my arm laid tense on his neck for a rein, hoping for river or ocean so he'll stop running, surprised by the chill of the water. But he reverses his path, goes back to the city. *Gardens* he must be thinking, deciding to leap a wall, black filigreed arrows barely visible under us, as his head comes up, as the front hooves rise, rise, then arc slow-motion back to the ground. An open gate, an alley, and he's off again, me clinging to his mane, delirious with fear. The river is somewhere to our left, I think, but no, we're swimming, he's swimming, me on his back, up to my waist in water so still it must be an inlet or bay protected from wind. When at last the moon emerges, I can see my face, far away, rippling, as if it were part of the other's, the horse's, wet body.

## French Bread

1 pkg. dry yeast
2 Tbsp. sugar
1 Tbsp. sea salt
2½ c. warm water
5–6 c. unbleached flour
sunflower oil
1 egg white with a little water added, for wash

*Bake at 450° for 15 minutes, 350° for 15 additional minutes.*
*Use two baguette pans, each divided into two parts.*

As if you were scattering seeds for wildflowers, toss dry yeast, sugar, sea salt, into a large white bowl. (Does the bowl *need* to be white? No, but it helps to imagine, against that background, eventual dark blossoms.) Bathe them in water, nearly hot, and let them come alive. It won't take long. Because, once begun, an organism wants to grow, add flour. Let your hands work it, like massaging silt into soil. But don't overdo. You want to keep it moist. You want it reluctant to leave your touch. Cover it closely and let it sleep in the sun for an hour or so. So nothing happens too fast, gently press the first swelling back. Then clear your mind. Contemplate as you separate what you've made into equal parts. Fit each to its own long bed, those beds soothed with sunflower oil. Here, in a pause, while you think, you may want to brush an egg-white wash on each one's skin. Cover—tight—and let them nap again while you nap too, and wait for the dream to repeat. Finally, uncover and let them have the heat they crave, spraying the oven with water to make it steam. After a while, reduce the heat and they won't burn. Released at last, they will have bloomed, their fragrance overwhelming all your rooms.

## *Labyrinths*

              What empties         the way
these nights do
       a blue current rippling through
         the life before the life
                   we entered with such ease
   it seemed
                 there must be no end
      what I read is made of longing    its author
               young
                  not knowing      yet what can go on
        even after

                   we

              even after

    everything
                     a labyrinth carved in snow
        blue snow

                         you arrive
            nothing said
               what we couldn't understand    we do
    the way in
        the way out

# *Discoveries in a Morning Diary*

But in those days my luck was good and more intriguing
    impulse taught what can and cannot
        it wasn't love for a change
       though certainly the pleasures of proximity      so underground
        I forget the path      no strings      no *Sturm und Drang*
the way a torch illuminates
      a cavern      enough to find the way out
        an exit in moonlight
    paradise      discovers you and keeps you
           will be forgotten too

  how a ruin      a balcony      a mountain
      record      I have learned to live
    without the promised treasure in the wall
          another century
    by the downstairs fire    the bedclothes piled    as a hand
      over me    quilts
  time the mind erases      humming alone
    on a spit
      we pull our clothes off
    three times before the lamb is done
  we lit the coals
    in sunlight
  I want to think about      conversations
      illuminated on a cave wall
      if you get cold      my side of the bed
of the brain
    it depends on who, doesn't it?

# Gratin Dauphinoise

1 garlic clove
3 lbs. baking potatoes, thinly sliced
1½ c. freshly grated Gruyère cheese
1½ c. crème fraîche or heavy cream
salt to taste

*Use 8 c. gratin dish. Bake at 350° for 1 hr.*

Think of the *pomme de terre*, earth apple, as the world's first, best temptation, and to better the story, let it contain a version of itself within itself. You're not in a garden, you're in a cabin by a lake. As you stand at the kitchen window, watching water ripple through pine shadows, cut the fragrant garlic clove in two. Then, on the bottom of your gratin dish, write a love letter with half the clove, answer with the other. It's fine if the words are invisible—who needs to read them can. Lay half the sliced potatoes in that shallow boat. Blanket them with half the cheese, half the cream, and salt. Think of this as Adam. Do the same with the other half for Eve. Let them lie together, to melt with pleasure, one into the other. Wrap them in towels and add them to your picnic basket, already filled with ham and pie and fruit. Put up your parasol and arrange yourself in the canoe, while your lover paddles and your friends glide next to you. At noon, on a nearby island, lay out a checkered cloth, the gratin still warm in its wrap. This marriage will delight your guests, while a snake hisses by, jealous of this usurpation of a tale, this heretic ambrosia, this perfection afloat in the world.

## *She Makes Another Comeback*

We're on our way to a gallery crawl, the halls clogged
with people in festive clothes, some of them dancing.
I hold my husband's arm and skip. He takes my cue
and kicks up his heels. We're as silly as just-met lovers. Until

I think of my mother in the nursing home, how fragile
she is, her mind half gone, how I wish my husband would offer,
on occasions like this, to bring her along.

When we arrive at the grand salon, there she is ahead of us,
in the arms of a man we've never met, and she's perfectly
naked. Somehow I'm not surprised. I observe again
how young her body is, in her eighties, hardly a wrinkle
on the taut white skin of her arms and legs.

Then she turns, and I notice the hair—long lush dark hair
that grows from her shoulders and torso,
though not on her breasts—she's Donatello's aged Magdalene,
whose long gray tresses are enmeshed in the goat pelt she wears.
Unlike Mother, the Magdalene covers her breasts
with frail, praying hands.

Now the man is holding my mother high
above the heads of the crowd, the way,
at a wine-rich feast among ancient Romans, a young man
might lift a beautiful girl in his arms, showing her off,
both in such high spirits
they can't help themselves.

# Dreams/Villages 4

### Esperaza

They are still digging, dinosaur bones piling up like the lies of lovers. This year, a new species. Its eggs trapped in silt are stone. Remember the way we imagined the future, blind to the slow hardening of possibility? Unearthing new knowledge, we must revise the reluctant past. Even a pale flame of a woman can grieve longer than anyone knows for her own petrified eggs, for a husband not deaf to her beauty, but mute. She stood here too, on the rim of this crater, watching the dig. She toured the museum where even the most surprising lives are arranged behind glass, classified.

### Mirepoix

In the square at midnight, one shop open, but no, they're only taking inventory, rugs and iron beds. Off the square, our favorite restaurant, its lights still on, the separate notes of a flute falling thin as centimes onto the dimming street. I turn another direction, and when I go back, Le Flambé too is closed, silent, everything black this starless night. A woman appears from the shadows of ancient trees, offers to lead me through the dark. We arrive at the old hotel, where upstairs I play blackjack into the early hours. I phone you, who arrive upset. We walk along the balustrade, centuries creaking wooden beneath us. Then find our room, a small white one, where I soothe you as the light gathers under the sash, beneath the moving curtain, light like snow, light rising through us into this hard-won life.

### Collioure

Two sides of the harbor sing to each other in different winds, like the voices of two boys of nearly identical age whose father is the same. One lives on the side with big houses, his a shining on the cliff, his father with him, making rhymes. His stately mother. They eat in the lantern-lit restaurant whose awnings are a ship's white sails from the other side, where the other child scrapes a fish for his supper. This seems a fairy tale from a different age, the bastard son, bare feet and toil, the young prince unaware, strolling the pier in velvet. But here they are at the end of the twentieth century, half-brothers who meet at school, play marbles, know the rumors, murmur the other's name in sleep, one's last sight in the night the man who reads to him, the other's the unsilvering mirror. We tell ourselves the unloved son will save himself as art saved others here. He might chant at dusk, where names drift on the sultry air: Braque, Matisse, Picasso, Derain, Collioure, Collioure.

## Someone Who Believes Herself Native

  *the land of my people*
 whose reserve  deliberately skidding cars
 (lamentations)  on the deep-frozen lake
whole lines of us  embroidering truth
  in our old Fords and Chevys  pushing the pedal down hard
 loops  intersecting with other loops spinning  Tilt-a-Whirls
  sobriety itself
  at the county fair  pumping calliopes  no maps
   back to long-grassed summer  and the skating rink
flooded pond in the middle of town  I spun on the serrated tips of blades
   and fell
 backward   jokes   cracking my head
  the warming shack air dense with steam  smelling wool
a dialect of sorts  those mittens and socks left
  on the woodstove to dry
 heard only the cracking  my first horse clutching the reins in both
mittened fists   slipping on snow-disguised ice
  after that
     the way fear stiffens
  from the banks of fjords to a land of lakes  gravity
   even bones
 glassed over  where fish swim below  over time
 in the dark  in the thickness of water as it hardens
  the magnet stronger
   specific earth I'd thought to leave behind
    pulled through a small ring of light
 breathing stops  in unaccustomed air  I chose something
  gasping for the proper element  continue to choose it

# Escaping the House of Certainty

Outdoor café in the mountains
under a warm October sun

peonies by the door
petals on the wing

Mother who comes back whole
married to a German

reading *Les Fleurs du Mal*
voice hovering low

bee at my ring
horse grazing my dreams

Mother
better than she's ever been

mind flexed
to learn Italian

now she swings on,
left foot in a stirrup

right leg over the saddle
cantering backward into snow

then out into spring.

# 3

I do not know him. *Take me home*,
he says, and we go to my childhood,
where my mother waits.
The grass beside the walk turns to water,
a lake; the man, a turtle.
I pull him out, lift him
to the window. My mother frowns
behind the glass. I lift him
to the window.

## *Amnesia*

And when we were turned out
of our houses, punishment for the fire
we'd set to keep warm,
they made us forget so that,
bereft, the pathways clouded over.
Under possible snow,
harbingers are lost. We sense
disturbance, mice playing brazenly,
cracks in the earth.

Traces on floors, kitchens that linger
all day nudge us to say, *no longer ours*.
Bones and fragments. We wanted someone
to take over our lives, wanted to be shaken.
We must go into the yard, what's buried be
retrievable. *Follow the stepping stones*.
No longer children in tents but bamboo
cold against our loneliness, shadows on bare feet,
the wind in bushes, stalks.
It was night. Loving acts, natural
of course, and not one was spared,
animals that we are.

## *The Family of Man*

        and woman        leaves
                                          frayed lines
            threads
                      invisible to the eye
the mind's wish        to slow time
        reverse cloud trails

        I'll call her Annie
                Osama's brother's mistress     American Annie
            tall and thin    teaching design in Paris
    turns the chalk sideways on the board
                draws
                        a naïve curl
    his shy daughter
        Annie's student in plain jeans
            will not accept a Mercedes
from her uncle                        1986
       bombs in the Hôtel de Ville   the Poste   a department store

  Drusilla's dining room     turquoise glass pales under fallen light
    the Shah's son next to me at dinner     those twilight eyes
        ignore his silken grandmother with her cane
            princess among women
in her son's reign      because of her
     our sisters    faces uncovered   had the vote
            princess
  older than the Russian peasant poet
    Medea        in sensible shoes
  Yugoslavia the year before
    a guard beside her in the car the restaurants the library
                outside her room
  *Ah   you Americans are like birds*      *you can fly anywhere you want*
        Radovan Karadzic not yet in flight
you may have heard me say it before   he was our guide   interpreter

what we are    no more than  six degrees    six people away they say
         from everyone  you too Reader    who know me as well as anyone

      imagine walking the corridors of Wilford Hall in San Antonio
                the Shah off balance    leaning on an arm
his ravaged face         no cruelty left
                  (I'm one away      you must be two)
      still handsome enough to turn the heads of nurses
            mine if I'd known him       maybe yours

      intuition could lead you to a cave in Serbia where you might
                fantasize that you'll prevail
            on Radovan          to walk
                  hands outstretched      into the Hague
      where he'll confess "some of the most heinous crimes
            of the twentieth century"    *Time* said
      (he was my friend in '84 so you're just one away from him)

            now on t.v. you see      someone like Jesus
those gentle hooded eyes       the striped robe
            head covered against the desert sun    Afghanistan
                leaning gracefully to whisper
   in a dream
            you'll reach to touch
                  his hand
                                    startled

                  by words
                      slow fire through a megaphone

            (I'm two away       you must be three)

      the world spins backward    *and the voice you hear*    *falling on your ear*
                  is no savior

                        the notes ring out from pipes
            of a childhood church

                splinter

    into strands
                    a web
                        after fire
                                after wind

## *Phantoms*
after a photograph by Julio Pimentel

We are so easy to fool.
Dress an angel in black and he seems
just another traveler waiting for a bus.
We forget that we too are in disguise,
wearing our heaviest days
until they become us.

Dry bread, undrinkable wine
in a dusty corner—
What we see, what we expect
to see.

Since we first discovered
the door to the cave, the last
we will enter,
we have misunderstood.

We have not noticed the robed figure
losing his head to radiance.

Nor the one who's come to sit
beside us on a bench,
no yearning in his posture,
bench and body
drenched in gold—

startle of breath
on our hair, whispered
intimation: here,
here is the shimmering world
within the world.

Friends, let us not be immune
to delight.

# *Christmas in the Officer's House*

Nights in the drift of December
    who is the third who is silent    the three of them
lie in the narrow bed
    dumb mounds in the moonlight        breathing
   his words    why she's always ready    the mattress astir
      the whisper in her      what is the meaning
 complained to his wife it's sure she'd never imagined him feeling
      he's thinking the same as I    so desperate
  poor men   poor her   all the night lonely bodies akindle
      why she'd dreamed of his nightstick
  while she slept at his elbow     defending her
 prowlers and drifters   she sleeps like a baby who hasn't yet felt
      dead to the world in the doorway
  something brush like a feather inside    but now it's not him
       despair relieving the ache    O god she must answer to
    if they were all alone     I wish I was old and he
       she said    it would
             all would be easier
      she'd open the doors     and so does he    so does
      the other to pleasure.     Who'd ever have known?

# Moroccan Tuna

*for each tuna steak (about 1½ inches thick):*

½ tsp. dried basil
½ tsp. dried thyme
½ tsp. dried oregano
¼ tsp. cinnamon
sea salt and white pepper to taste
1 tsp. fresh lemon juice
1 tsp. olive oil
1 tsp. melted butter
1 tsp. crushed coriander seeds

Ah, the spices of the Orient. How we've dreamed of them, imagined ships with yellow sails that carried cinnamon and seeds, carried the means for changing us. (When we look in the mirror, whom do we think we'll see?) Along with salt and pepper, we grind the herbs and cinnamon into sultry powders and mix them up to conjure with. Then massage them into each body (the tuna's, not our own) until the fish glow. Sprinkle lemon juice and oil. Imagine the broiler is the sun, late afternoon, and we are giving already golden skin a darker sheen. Place them 4 inches from the heat, 3 minutes for each side, and they'll maintain their pink and tender parts inside, reminding us, if we wish to be reminded, that we're still ourselves underneath. If we don't want to remember, we might cook them longer. Last, we'll brush with melted butter, sprinkle with coriander, serve with couscous. By now we'll be wearing silk, will have darkened our eyes with kohl. The oil lamps will be burning blue. We'll count on what we've always heard: you are what you eat. For a while it will seem true.

# Barcelona, the Spanish Civil War
## ALFONSO LAURENCIC INVENTS TORTURE BY ART

Flogged by color and its cubist cousins—not
what Klee and Kandinsky had in mind, but genius
breeds genius. The body can be made to lose
its recollections born in music, its desire for bread
and sex, its only wish confession. How easily
the brain opens its many mouths to red.

The freakish sun weeps through green panes
into a tiny cell tarred inside and out to magnify heat,
a plank bed is angled to prevent sleep, nowhere to look
but the walls spiraling the viewer into nausea.

The sublime rides a pogo stick, vaults
beyond ridiculous, beyond heinous—

What luck—a prisoner might crawl into Buñuel's
giant eye torn by a razor, disappear
through that ragged hole into
the mind of the maker.

## *We Do Not Notice*

      a mist is falling through the roof

            the whole room under the spray
          everyone
        surprised             distressed by the rain
    seeping through      into the room

      in the bedroom

a doctor
    is nursing someone through her last moments,
  a woman in a fringed skirt
   she is sweating   the doctor is sweating   he has his arm
around her back he is trying to help she says let me go there's nothing
   he does   she contorts   her body fills   bright blood rises
we're still

     at the table

        does everyone live with a cloud like a roof?

## *Again the Thickness of the Night*

        too much certainty
      describes                 the hours the spider's web unravels
and you who understand      the dangers
                        scheme abandon and gardens

     what has gone barren
         suspects the ancient never speaks
              but shows itself      gods and men in daylight lapses

     abandons us to drift
                when certain names are spoken
dreamless knowledge         fever more acute in
                          forests we have not walked
        the starry world at broken intervals
           we'd choose years and all our loves asleep     we'd see
    a wild      more ominous
                join the silent chorus
       uncertainty         the desperate dust

## *I Thought I Knew You*

      the strangest thing        age makes
          tumble through the brain

       you cross
                     the locks
            a hanging bridge
sways      you knew
     the combination to the river    so far down
               it's a soft fall
  click
      the way an incident
in this wind from long ago        suddenly a note
       you know you can't hear    and anything
could happen
  it would have made you thrill    too dizzy to move    now
                you walk on trust  a single bell ringing
      all these years I thought
you could fix your eyes on the mountain
     seem almost nonchalant
    think        it will not be today

# *Bin Laden in South Carolina*

It is equal to living in a tragic land
To live in a tragic time.
      —Wallace Stevens

We are strolling near the forest when we spot him.
You aim your rifle, he puts his hands up so slowly
he seems to be starting to dance, a dance that begins
in his graceful fingers.

We march him to our house in the meadow,
to the back yard where you tie him
to a chair.

I bring him books. *Bind his wrists if you must,*
I plead, *but please leave his hands free enough
to turn the pages.* You do not acknowledge
that you've heard me.
I shrug in his direction, reassuring.

I wonder if he reads English.
*He must be bored,* I say, *sitting in the sun
for hours.* I think of lemonade,
cold beer. You growl at me,
*It's you who have been in the sun too long.*

My family comes to visit. They enter the yard
through the gate, a stream of them
carrying casseroles, steaming pies.
As they pass him I whisper who he is.
*Don't stare,* I say. *You especially,* I hiss
to Aunt Helen, who does. They all do,
peeking from behind a curtain.
He sees them. He lowers his limpid eyes.

I peer out the window, against the rising sun.
Gone, I think with a pang.
But I'm wrong. His head lifts
from the damp grass. The chair
must have fallen,
he's only been sleeping.

I suggest a more comfortable chair,
offer to go get a cushion.
You stalk behind him, pushing
the barrel into the small of his back.

Your voice is harsh, reminding me
you were a soldier. You show me the stash
of knives hid in the folds of his robe,
tell me the ropes look loose, I should fix them.
I avert my eyes.

*Do you find him handsome*, my mother asks,
appearing beside me.
*Oh yes*, I say, settling his feet
in the grass, retying the knots.
His hands lie still in his lap.

What more can I do?

Who is responsible? Whom shall we call?
You raise the rifle to your shoulder,
bend to the sight,
tell me to move aside.

## 4

Then come broken lakes, fish shadows slow among the floes, and finally green that makes them sing, arrival the occasion for high trembling notes, no matter what follows.

# *Danse Macabre*
### after photographs by Connie Imboden

## I. THE BEGINNING
## "Dead Silences"

In the beginning
              was the body         dreaming
                                arms raised
                    as if to say                 there are no
                             barriers
                                        as if to say
       here I am

nipples say so too
                       if the mask
             has two faces                     here
  they are twins          the same
                    vision floating through

      neither comic nor tragic

                  my face says

this is the only place
        there is                          I am drifting in a pool
                   at midnight
             you are invisible
                in the shadows
                 there is no
             speech between us
                  no music
Only this
                darkness and light
                   two worlds
                     one

## "Disintegration"

        Underwater        the torso takes on

            features of face

                contours of skull

the anthropologist's dream        nipple-eyes intact

        though the nose is broken off

                as we'd expect        like the stone Diana

        moldering in Saint-Germain-en-Laye


      the mind        housed in the body        becomes one

with it

    tentacles

        reaching everywhere


                I feel my fingers

   tingle        as thought

slips from the shallows

        into a deeper pool


the mouth is a cave        of lipless surprise

    at this cold glimpse

        of the future


        thought disengages

            suddenly my arm

                is someone else's

        a foreign

            expanse of flesh so close

it's magnified        some other creature

    maybe            denuded


  the body continues its slide

      begins to turn        a *danse macabre*

erasing culture        though some

            will see a literal descent

  in what the soul comes to know

    here        when metaphor fails

                    my own history tumbles
        backward into a choir loft
                        in a cold season
                the startle goes through spine
            to breast         another
    turn                            and it's my brain            blinking
                        an eye stares out
                terrified

                    heart              where are you

## II. DARK NIGHT OF THE SOUL

## "Untitled"

    she is sleeping
                        he is the dream
                        hovering over her
                        his head bends
                            to her neck
            leaning back
                        in what might be
                                        ecstasy
                    he might be demon
                        holding her down
                                    he might be savior
                            lifting her into his arms


if there is fear
                        it has not yet devoured us
                        in the fullness of our flesh
                        he surrounds us
                        his mottled arms caressing ours

        we start to take on
                            his heaviness
                    we do not know
where he is taking us

    he might be whispering
                                    lies        or assurances
                          true as the place
                                where she finds herself

we want to be saved
                                          pulled from these depths        but
   his hand opens                  that gesture
                              swearing
                                                                           innocent

        whatever he's saying
                                  bent to her
             in the crosshatch of leaves
       and hair                                          of night
              and twilight        she is listening

he turns to look up
              then back

                          to the willing throat
             a shadow
when she wakes
                         if she wakes
                she will know
                      what she did not know

quick     there is still time
                                our plump arms
          our breasts     say so

## III. THE LIGHT RESEEN

### "Untitled"

can it be true     as I heard someone say
                          that desire
                                  is the first apprehension

                              once I saw myself Ahab

                                            but now it's the whale
I see stretched to a single pulsating line
                an eel      arc of silver                    electric

             think of matter become
                              an Einsteinian thought
                                            endings trailing off
                                                            as daydream
                              undulations of flesh
                                     remind us what travels
                                                    at the speed of speech


                     light pure as grace
ascending backward
                              is it the power of denial
                                I'm attracted to

        I think

                              it's the impulse to swim
                                            to where there is no bottom
                              to take into myself
                                            the surrounding darkness

what we are is music
                              so singular all we can hear
                                     is luminosity        curved and stretched
                              one distance to another

risk is reason
                              who would have needed to ask
                                     about Everest

           dive and drift
                              fin and wing
                                            I admonish myself
                     there are patterns you cannot enter
           but the body can be made

to will itself out of one world into another
it has no certain knowledge of
no memory

## IV. THE BODY REFORMED

## "Untitled"

now what's left is what we used
    to fantasize                           body minus mind.

mouths remain       and breasts
                    whose weight is buoyed by desire
          a man's arm circles her
          her belly rests on his shoulder

the hair on his torso is thick
                    as weeds

they might be gilled
              they are so at home
                in the deep
    we'd slip into the slow spin of fish
          as they spiral         facing each other

an onlooker might not be able
      to tell if this were a challenge
        to duel         that erotic choreography
          or the invitation
we humans make when we're

    speechless         caught in waves
        in the dark     unable to say
        who we are

        who we are
    arc shapes against space
          fragments afloat in the universe

## V. PERFECT BEAUTY

### "Sacred Silences"

whose hand is cradled
                in a soft shell of skin

you might think         at a glance
                is vagina

        a scar leads up
   to say
        here a child was born
           I have been that splitting
          the signs remain imprinted
         on my belly
the human hand   can anything
        be more tender
                But

hands hide fear and shame
      leftover clutches of the heart
   that no longer knows         where it belongs

    once I thought of erasing
        those jagged lines
      with surgery     but then I said
     no       I need maps
    of the past             markers of paths
      that do not disappear
        as the years crowd in

      what is perfection
    in a world where everything
         changes so quickly

                even my body feels
      lost
    in the cities it knew best

                once this was my definition
                hands folded in prayer
                    and below

                                everything opening
              we sense we are moving
                            toward something
      not unspeakable
                                  *unsayable*

              my hands tremble with words
                          they press back
                                  into my mouth
        while the elements I understand

                            are in clear focus

            in time you will not recognize
                          the parts of you that might be me
            I will not know
            myself

in the moon-spliced wake
                of a century's hard turning
      I call to a place in between
            where breath leaves the body
                        invisible
            taking a white-petaled lane
                                  in the direction of spirit